Sandra Markle

The Case of the
Vanishing Honeybees

A Scientific Mystery

M Millbrook Press . Minneapolis

For Curious Children Everywhere!

Acknowledgments: The author would like to thank the following people for taking the time to share their expertise: Dr. May Berenbaum, Professor and Head of Entomology Department, University of Illinois at Urbana–Champaign; Dr. R. W. (Rob) Currie, Professor and Head of Entomology Department, University of Manitoba; Dr. Gloria DeGrandi-Hoffman, Research Leader, United States Department of Agriculture, Agricultural Research Service, Carl Hayden Bee Research Center; Dr. Keith Delaplane, Professor and Program Director, College of Agricultural & Environmental Sciences, University of Georgia; Dr. John Hafernik, Professor, Department of Biology, San Francisco State; David Hackenberg; Randy Oliver; Susan Olson; Dr. Jeffery Pettis, Bee Research Leader, United States Department of Agriculture–Agricultural Research Service; and Dr. Marla Spivak, Professor, University of Minnesota. A special thank-you to Skip Jeffery for his loving support during the creative process.

Text Copyright © 2014 by Sandra Markle

Main body text set in Johnston ITC Std. 14/21.
Typeface provided by International Typeface Corp.

Millbrook Press
A division of Lerner Publishing Group, Inc.
241 First Avenue North
Minneapolis, MN 55401 U.S.A.

Website address: www.lernerbooks.com

Library of Congress Cataloging-in-Publication Data

Markle, Sandra.
    The case of the vanishing honeybees : a scientific mystery / by Sandra Markle.
        p.   cm
    Includes index.
    ISBN 978-1-4677-0592-9 (lib. bdg. : alk. paper)
    ISBN 978-1-4677-1700-7 (eBook)
    1. Honeybee—Health—Juvenile literature. 2. Honeybee—Juvenile literature. I. Title.
  SF538.M37 2014
  595.79'9—dc23   2012046913

Manufactured in the United States of America
1 – PC – 7/15/13

Table of Contents

It's a Mystery

On a warm day in October 2006, Dave Hackenberg went to check on his workers. Hackenberg is a beekeeper, and his workers are millions of honeybees. As he walked among a group of nearly four hundred beehives, he expected to see the air full of bees. It wasn't. Curious, Hackenberg lifted the cover of one hive and peeked inside. Three weeks earlier, when he drove this group of beehives to Florida from Pennsylvania, each hive was home to about thirty thousand bees. Now he found only the bee colony's egg-laying queen and her brood (developing young) inside the hive. Thousands of worker bees were missing.

Dave Hackenberg checks on a few of his 3,200 beehives.

Worried, Hackenberg checked dozens more hives. He discovered they were nearly empty too. But there weren't any dead bees to be found inside the hives or on the ground around the hives. In his fifty years as a beekeeper, Hackenberg had never seen anything quite like this.

What had happened to all the bees?

This is a section of a beehive after the workers disappeared and the untended brood died.

If Honeybees Are in Trouble, We're in Trouble!

Having insects such as honeybees vanish may not seem like a big deal, but it is. Without honeybees, you could be limited to eating oats, rice, and corn. These foods come from plants that use wind to move their pollen (male reproductive cells) to their ovules (female reproductive cells). The process of transferring pollen is called pollination. It has to happen for a plant to produce seeds, parts that contain an embryo, or baby plant. That's how the plant produces more of its own kind of plant. The wind pollinates some plants. But birds, bats, and insects, especially bees, pollinate many more. Honeybees, in particular, are needed in order to grow apples, raspberries, watermelon, almonds, and cucumbers—to name just a few.

These are some of the foods you can enjoy thanks to honeybees.

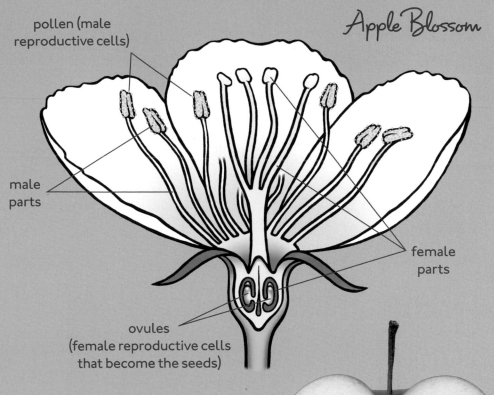

pollen (male
reproductive cells)

Apple Blossom

male
parts

female
parts

ovules
(female reproductive cells
that become the seeds)

Honeybees depend on plants just as plants depend on bees. Many plants produce nectar, a sweet liquid, to attract bees and other pollinators. Bees gather this liquid as food. The nectar's scent attracts bees to a plant. Many flowers are also colored to signal that they contain nectar. The flowers are shaped to make sure that visiting honeybees will spread pollen in return for the food.

To reach nectar, a worker bee usually has to burrow into a flower. The bee brushes past the flower's male parts, where it collects pollen, and the female parts, containing the plant's ovules. The bee picks up pollen this way and also drops off a little pollen, often from another flower. To form a seed, the ovules and the pollen must be from the same kind of plant. Fortunately, honeybees tend to visit only one kind of plant during a nectar-collecting flight. And each flower produces just a few drops of nectar a day. So during each flight, a bee visits as many as four hundred flowers. That's a lot of pollination!

Only flowers that are pollinated produce fruit.

Back at the hive, the worker passes the nectar it collected to another bee. That bee uses its strawlike mouthpart to pump the nectar into a cell in the hive's wax comb (wall of wax cells). The nectar mixes with the bee's digestive juices. Then lots of worker bees join in fanning their wings. This increases airflow over the nectar mixture in the cells. Nectar straight from the flower is as much as 80 percent water. Airflow causes some of the water to evaporate (move into the air). But doing this just once isn't enough. Another bee sucks up the liquid and repeats the process. Little by little, the nectar becomes a sugar-rich, thick liquid—honey.

Bees eat honey for energy to fly and stay active. Any extra is stored in the hive's cells and capped with wax. The bees will eat this honey later, when plants aren't flowering and producing nectar.

Between flights, this worker bee passes its nectar load, mouth to mouth, to another worker.

Bees get more food from a plant than just the nectar. They use the plant's pollen too. While bees are sucking up nectar, pollen sticks to them. They regularly comb pollen off their bodies and pack it into basketlike parts on their hind legs. Some pollen

pollen

A bee's hind legs have a cuplike shape surrounded by stiff, curved hairs. These act like little baskets for carrying pollen grains.

brushes off on other flowers. There's always some left over, though, when the bees return to the hive. Each returning bee backs into one of the empty wax cells on the comb and flicks off the pollen.

Other workers chew the pollen, mixing it with a little honey. That turns the pollen into beebread, a high-protein food bees need to stay strong and healthy.

As you can see, the partnership between bees and plants is important to life for both. Without plants producing nectar and pollen, bees wouldn't have food. And without bees visiting the flowers to collect nectar, many plants wouldn't be able to reproduce. This partnership benefits another group too—people!

In January 2007, beekeepers in the United States met. Many had experienced losses like Dave Hackenberg's. They named the mysterious loss of their bees Colony Collapse Disorder, or CCD. By then it was clear this wasn't a local problem or even just limited to the United States. There were reports of bee colonies collapsing in many countries around the world. Beekeepers everywhere were losing about 30 percent of their hives. In some places, the reported losses were as high as 50 percent.

Beekeepers learn to look for signs, such as shrinking numbers of worker bees, that could mean their bee colonies are in danger of collapse.

This was a bigger issue than beekeepers losing business. Without honeybees, some food crops would fail. People could go hungry.

Like beekeepers, scientists joined forces to tackle CCD. Everyone agreed the worker bees must be dying, not just leaving their hives. Only death could keep honeybee workers from returning to their colony.

So what could be killing the bees?

There were few dead bees to provide clues about what happened.

All in the Family

The beekeeper marks the queen bee to make her easy to spot in the hive. The beekeeper watches the queen to be sure she is healthy and producing eggs.

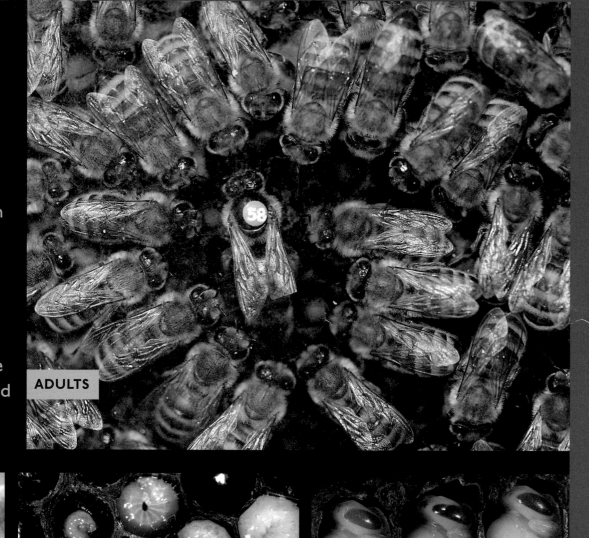

ADULTS

EGG

LARVAE

PUPAE

During its lifetime, a honeybee goes through complete metamorphosis. That means each stage of its development looks and behaves differently. Bees go through four stages: egg, larva, pupa, and adult.

Why Are Worker Bees So Important?

A honeybee hive is a colony made up of twenty thousand to thirty thousand adult bees. Most of these are worker bees. However, a honeybee colony is more than just a group of bees living together. It's a family.

The mother of the colony is the queen. She's the only female able to produce offspring. She produces about two thousand eggs each day. Adding new young to the colony is her only job. Workers constantly hover around her, feeding her and carrying her wastes out of the hive.

The colony also has a few hundred to a few thousand drones. These are males that are able to reproduce. Their only job is to mate with any new queen bees the hive produces. (Even though they may live up to five years, honeybee queens mate only shortly after they become adults.) Drones are raised during the summer. Any still in the hive in the fall are usually pushed out by the workers. The drones soon die.

Thousands of worker bees make up the rest of the colony. These are females that can't produce offspring. Worker bees perform lots of very important jobs for the colony. What a worker does depends on her age.

This worker is feeding larvae. Larvae need to eat and grow a lot in just five days to be ready to change into adult bees.

A worker's first job as an adult is housecleaning. Worker bees clear out empty cells that were used to raise young, called larvae, in the hive. Then these cells can be reused to raise more brood.

By the time a worker has been an adult for about four days, she's able to digest pollen and produce a special liquid called brood food. It's fed to the larvae. The young workers also produce an especially rich brood food called royal jelly. They feed it to the queen bee and take care of her for the next week of their lives. Workers also feed royal jelly to some of the larvae. These will develop into new queen bees.

A young worker bee can also produce wax. So she's able to help repair wax cells and build new ones for the hive. The cells are used to store beebread and honey as well as to rear brood.

Bees take wax flakes from other bees and chew them. Then they use their mouthparts to shape the wax into six-sided, tubelike cells. These become the hive.

WAX

When a worker bee is about two weeks old, she goes to the hive entrance to meet returning foragers (bees that have been collecting nectar). She connects mouthparts with a forager and receives its nectar. Then her job is to make and store honey. She also makes and stores beebread.

When she's about three weeks old, the worker leaves the hive on her first flight. She spends the rest of her life, about three more weeks, as a forager.

During every life stage, a worker bee's jobs are essential to the colony's survival. Without workers, the colony collapses.

These worker bees are ferrying nectar and pollen to the hive.

What Is Killing the Honeybees?

Could It Be a Change in Habitat?

Could honeybees be dying because something in their habitat, the place they live, changed? The sources of pollen and nectar available to honeybees have changed a lot. Farms were once a patchwork of fields growing a variety of different crops. Many modern farms have acres and acres devoted to a single crop. Bee researcher Jeff Pettis sees this as a problem for bees. "When local bees only have corn available," he said, "they have to fly as far as 5 miles [8 kilometers] from the hive to go beyond the corn and find enough sources of nectar. That wears out their wings and shortens their lives." Pettis believes the way the bees' habitat has changed could be a reason why colonies are vanishing.

Since wind usually pollinates corn, corn plants don't need to attract bees. Corn plants produce no nectar.

Homes close together with small lawns aren't bee-friendly places.

In many places, cities cover areas where there were once meadows full of wildflowers. Streets, parking lots, office buildings, shopping centers, and homes leave little room for plants. This is another way honeybees have lost some of their sources of nectar and pollen.

Could Honeybees Be Overworked?

Scientists wondered if bees could be dying from being pushed to work year-round. When honeybees live in just one place, there is often a season when little or nothing is blooming. During that period, bees don't work to collect nectar and pollen. Instead, they rest and live off their stored food. The queen also takes a break from producing eggs.

However, honeybees often do not just live in one place. Farmers on big farms and orchards rent large numbers of bees from beekeepers. To pollinate all their crops, these farmers need more bees than they could raise on their own. So beekeepers load their beehives onto trucks and move

Once the beehives are loaded onto the truck, they're covered. This keeps the bees inside the hives during transport.

them from place to place as they are needed. That's good business for beekeepers. It also means farmers can produce lots of food for people. But it means the bees no longer have as much time to rest.

A Year in the Life of a Traveling Honeybee Colony

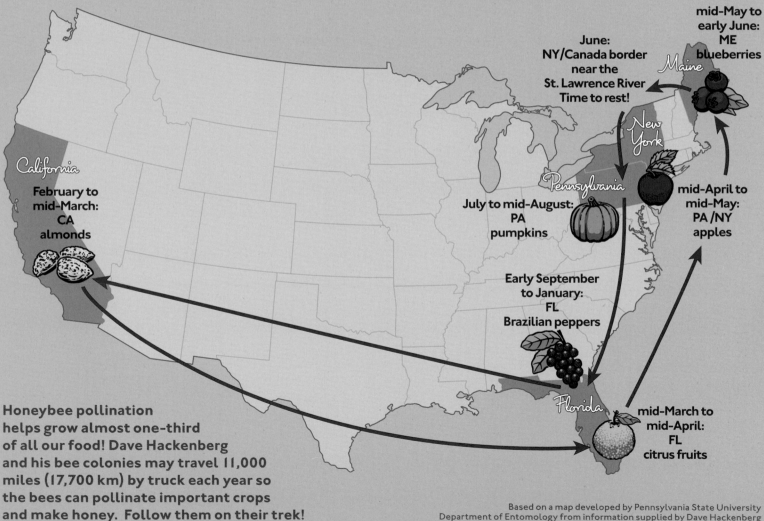

mid-May to
early June:
ME
blueberries

June:
NY/Canada border
near the
St. Lawrence River
Time to rest!

Maine

New York

Pennsylvania

mid-April to
mid-May:
PA /NY
apples

California

February to
mid-March:
CA
almonds

July to mid-August:
PA
pumpkins

Early September
to January:
FL
Brazilian peppers

Florida

mid-March to
mid-April:
FL
citrus fruits

Honeybee pollination helps grow almost one-third of all our food! Dave Hackenberg and his bee colonies may travel 11,000 miles (17,700 km) by truck each year so the bees can pollinate important crops and make honey. Follow them on their trek!

Based on a map developed by Pennsylvania State University
Department of Entomology from information supplied by Dave Hackenberg

19

Together, the almond orchards of California's Central Valley cover an area as large as the state of Rhode Island.

California's annual almond crop is a good example of the need for transporting bees. The almond blossom season, starting in early February, is the single biggest pollination event in the world. Over one million beehives are needed for about four weeks. Having lots of bees on hand is the only way orchard owners can make sure nearly all the flowers on their almond trees will be pollinated and their trees will produce large numbers of almonds. The resulting nut crop is about 80 percent of the world's almonds—a $3-billion-a-year industry.

Beekeepers earn big money by having their bees work in the almond orchards. To have their hives rented, though, it's not enough for them to be available when the almond farmers need the bees. The hives must also have booming populations of worker bees.

But scientist Gloria DeGrandi-Hoffman sees problems when the bees are moved. She explains, "Beekeepers are moving their colonies to almond orchards as early as November." Because there aren't any flowers nearby at that point, the bees are fed a diet of sugar syrup. This is cheaper than honey, and while it gives the bees the same sort of high-energy food, it's not the same. "Workers raised on sugar syrup are weaker," DeGrandi-Hoffman says. "Transporting the bees so early gives two strikes against them. They miss their natural rest and they don't get the nutrition they need to work." Those two factors could be enough to cause colonies to collapse.

A hive won't be rented unless, like this one, it has at least eight frames (hanging sections) covered with active worker bees.

One Suspect Cleared

Some researchers thought wide use of cell phones was to blame for CCD. They thought all the wireless communication somehow interfered with a bee's natural ability to navigate. So workers couldn't find their way home and would fly until they died.

To test this idea, cell phones and audio recorders were put inside five beehives. When the cell phones were active, playing music, the bees made the sounds they make when getting ready to swarm (fly away to start a new colony).

"But this test wasn't realistic," said scientist May Berenbaum. "Cellphones wouldn't usually be that close to the bees. Also, even though the bees made those sounds, they didn't swarm."

Other scientists agreed that cell phones weren't to blame for the bees' disappearance.

According to the Cellular Telecommunications and Internet Association (CTIA), as early as 2011, the number of wireless devices in use in the United States was more than the number of people living there. Imagine the number worldwide!

Could Mites Be the Killer?

Varroa mites attach themselves to a bee and suck its blood. This doesn't usually kill the bee, but it weakens the bee and shortens its life. The mite's bite often also passes on viruses, disease-causing living things, to the bee. Because the bee is already weak from the mite's attack, a virus might kill it.

Once varroa mites are in a hive, they reproduce and their numbers rapidly multiply. It's no wonder the mites spread quickly through the bee colony. The varroa mites also spread to other hives when nectar is scarce and bees from one colony come to steal honey from another hive.

Varroa mites are a big problem for honeybees. However, efforts to prevent varroa mite attacks are causing even more trouble. May Berenbaum explains, "Beekeepers put massive amounts of chemicals into their hives to protect the bees from varroa mites. Those chemicals can also be hard on the bees."

Berenbaum believes varroa mites and the chemicals used to protect bees from them could be at least part of what's causing CCD.

The varroa mite, a cousin of a spider, has been nicknamed the vampire mite for sucking bloodlike liquid from bees.

MITE

Could a Deadly Fungus Be Killing Honeybees?

A fungus called *Nosema ceranae*, a distant relative of bread mold, is another problem for honeybees. It spreads when an infected bee stops at puddles and ponds for a drink and drops its wastes. The seedlike spores from this fungus can be left there. If a healthy bee drinks that water, it may take in some of the spores. Then the fungus begins to grow in the bee's gut. This affects the lining of the honeybee's digestive system. The cells of the lining no longer produce the juices the bee needs to digest its food. So the bee doesn't get the energy it needs to be active. And instead of leaving the hive to drop its wastes, the infected bee drops some wastes inside the hive. Then other bees in the hive pick up the spores and become infected too.

A bee infected with *Nosema ceranae* becomes weak. It may become too weak to make it back to the hive from a foraging trip. But scientists and beekeepers can't easily tell when the fungus is at work. Bee researcher Rob Currie says, "The problem is that, with *Nosema ceranae*, there aren't any obvious symptoms."

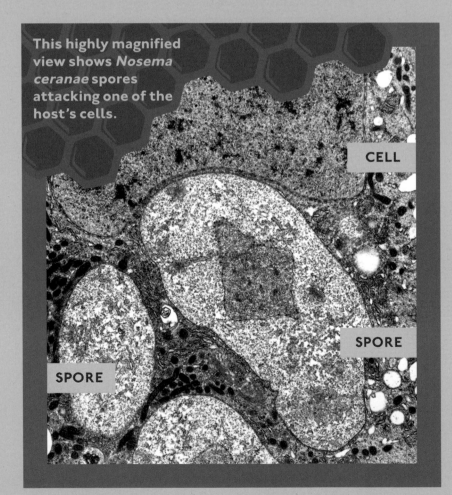

This highly magnified view shows *Nosema ceranae* spores attacking one of the host's cells.

CELL

SPORE

SPORE

The only way beekeepers or researchers can be sure that this fungus is what's causing workers to disappear is to examine some of the bees in a colony. They squash bee bodies and study them through a microscope to check for the fungi's spores. Like bees attacked by varroa mites, bees with *Nosema ceranae* often fall victim to viruses. Then it's the viruses that kill the bees.

Currie believes honeybees being infected with both *Nosema ceranae* and viruses could be a key reason colonies are collapsing.

This bee didn't have any symptoms to show it was sick before it died.

Could Pesticides Be the Problem?

Chemicals called pesticides are used to kill plants, animals, and fungi that attack plant leaves and fruit. However, many pesticides, especially those used to kill insect pests, are also harmful to people. So in the mid-1990s, farmers around the world switched to using newer chemicals called neonicotinoid pesticides. These were developed to mimic nicotine, a chemical found in a tobacco plant's leaves. It acts on insects' nervous systems to paralyze the insects and then kill them.

The new chemicals were designed to be safe for people and animals other than insects. Scientists also believed neonicotinoids were safe for bees, even though they are insects. That's because bees were only exposed to small doses while collecting nectar and pollen from flowers. By 2009, though, many beekeepers and scientists around the world agreed that small doses may be all that's needed to harm honeybees. Gloria DeGrandi-Hoffman's research team is studying how even small doses of chemicals may affect bees.

She believes exposure to pesticides might be at least partly to blame for bee deaths and colony losses.

Helicopters spray pesticides over large areas, like this almond orchard.

Tiny tracking devices let researchers follow foraging bees to study them.

Honeybee Killer—Case Open

Clearly, a lot of different things could be killing honeybees. Scientist Keith Delaplane said, "We're conditioned to think one problem means one cure, but we're discovering the world is more complicated than that."

No one yet knows what combination of causes is killing entire colonies of honeybees. So researchers are continuing to study bees to better understand how their bodies function. Researchers are also continuing to study how bees work together as a colony. Meanwhile, beekeepers and people who simply want to help are doing what they can. The goal is to keep honeybees alive while scientists search for a way to stop CCD.

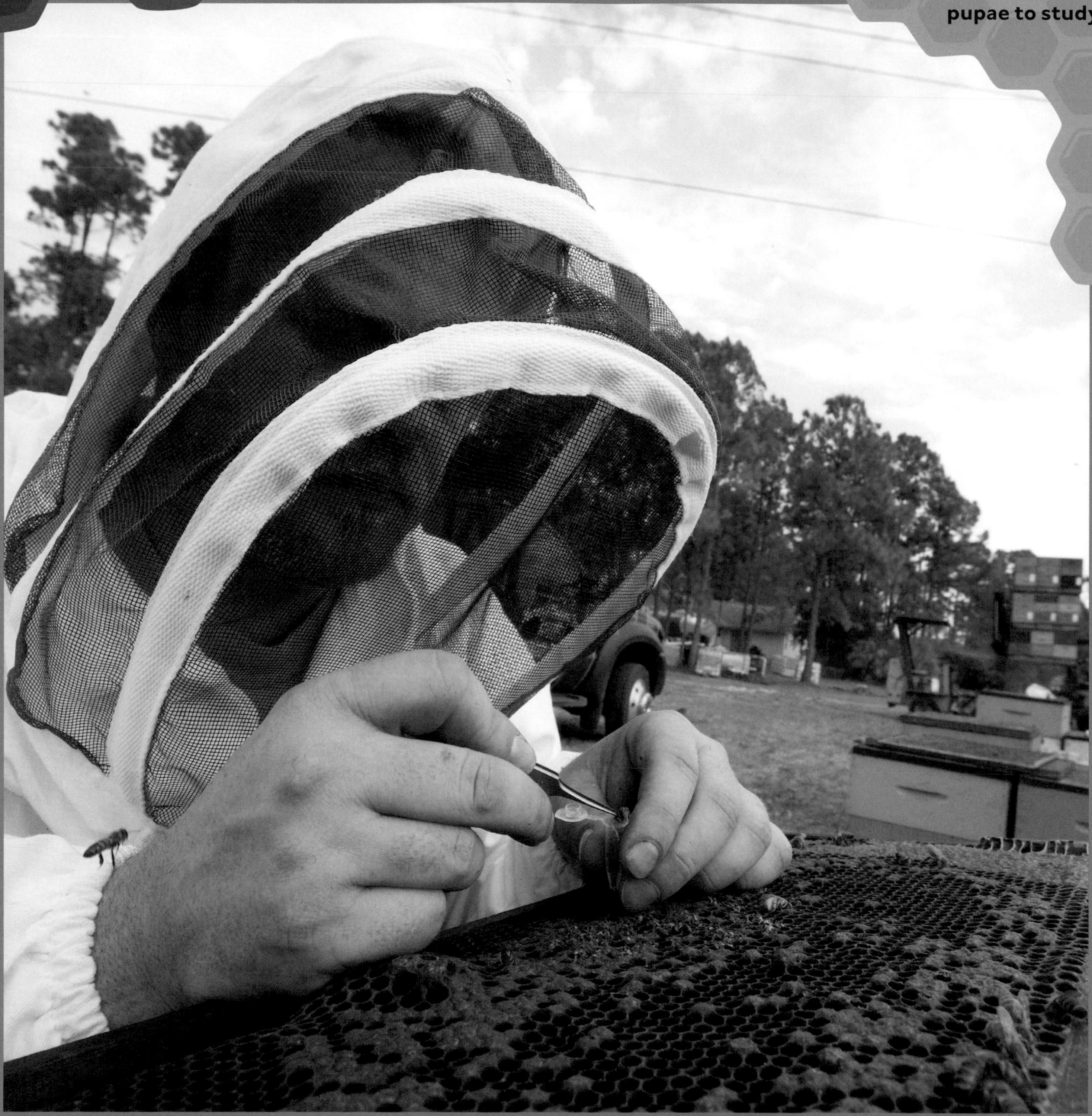

This scientist is collecting bee pupae to study.

Two Lucky Things about Bees

The impact of CCD could be even worse if not for two lucky facts about bees. First, hives can be split so one hive becomes two. Second, honeybees can easily be moved and will quickly adapt to pollinating plants wherever they are living.

Beekeepers have always been able to replace lost hives fairly easily, as research Jeff Pettis explained. "If you lost one of two dairy cows, you couldn't split the remaining cow in half and have two again. However, you can do that with a bee colony, because colonies produce a number of new queen bees each year."

To split a colony, half the worker bees are moved to a new hive. Next, a new queen bee that has mated and is ready to start laying eggs is introduced to that new hive. Then, over time, each new colony will raise enough young to grow into a full colony.

This is a swarm of bees. Sometimes, bee colonies just naturally split to form two colonies from one.

As long as they aren't overworked, bees can be moved. Then they will take over doing the same work that local bees did previously. Beekeeper Randy Oliver has seen this. "Moving bees from crop to crop is like moving cows or sheep to fresh pastures," he said. "Once the bees are relocated, we uncover the hives. Even before the last bees are released, the first colonies are out foraging."

Released after a long trip, the bees leave to drop their wastes. Honeybees don't usually drop wastes inside their hives.

Give Bees a Healthy Diet

Gloria DeGrandi-Hoffman realized a bee's diet was also a major player in CCD. "I believed many problems that developed—even CCD—were downstream effects of poor nutrition," she said. "So my team developed a special bee diet."

Now beekeepers can feed their bees this high-protein diet instead of sugar syrup. That keeps the worker bees strong and healthy while they're waiting for a crop such as almonds to bloom.

To prove this new diet would help bees stay healthy and colonies survive, DeGrandi-Hoffman's team set up twin flight arenas. These were screened areas where bee colonies could live but not escape. One group was given a solution of sugar syrup to feed on. Another was given the new protein-rich food. At first, both groups did well. However, bees fed on sugar syrup started foraging at a younger age and died sooner than those fed the protein-rich diet.

These bees are being fed a sugar syrup diet.

Using computer modeling, DeGrandi-Hoffman's team also projected what would happen if varroa mites attacked. The results were that the colony feeding on sugar syrup wouldn't be able to replace workers fast enough. So the colony would collapse. What honeybees eat clearly makes a difference.

These bees are sucking up the special protein-rich drink.

As news about CCD spread around the world, people everywhere became concerned that a loss of honeybees could seriously affect plant pollination. Soon people who had never before considered tending bees started taking action. To make sure there were plenty of bee colonies in their area, they set up beehives near their homes. The idea of beekeeping even caught on in big cities.

These beehives have been on the roof of the Paris Opera House for nearly twenty years.

Today there are beehives on house rooftops, on apartment building balconies, on school grounds, and even on the grounds of famous landmarks.

The air around city buildings is usually warmer than the surrounding area. That's good for bees in parts of the world where winters can be cold. And in every city where bees are given homes, plants benefit from having resident pollinators. People who tend honeybees get a treat too—the honey that the bees produce.

A beehive was installed at the White House in 2009. With lots of gardens around it, it has produced as much as 340 pounds (154 kg) of honey in a year—nearly twice what hives normally produce.

37

Raise Hygienic Bees

Researcher Marla Spivak and her team help breed a special kind of bee that's helping colonies survive. These are called hygienic bees. (When something is clean enough to be healthy, it's said to be hygienic.) Hygienic bees fight back when varroa mites and some diseases attack their hive. Scientists have discovered that sick pupae or pupae infested with mites give off odors. Hygienic worker bees can detect those smells with their antennae. When the workers identify a pupa with those odors, they kill it. Then they remove it from the hive, keeping the colony clean. That's why they're called hygienic.

How does Spivak breed these special bees? She explained, "I tracked colonies that were good honey producers and showed hygienic behavior. Then I used them to raise queens. It took about six years, but I finally developed queens that would produce hygienic colonies."

Now beekeepers can raise colonies that can defend themselves against mites and some diseases. The colonies of hygienic bees are raised close to other hygienic bee colonies. That way, any new queens will naturally mate with hygienic drones. Then the new colonies those queens start will carry on that special trait.

The queen is inside a cage sealed with a candy plug. It will take a couple of days for worker bees to eat through this plug and release her. That's time enough for them to get used to her pheromones (chemical signals) and accept her.

The worker bees tear the mite-infested pupa into small pieces and carry those out of the hive.

39

Give Bees a Break

Eric and Sue Olson, beekeepers for thirty-five years, decided to try giving their bees a winter break. They knew they had to do something, or CCD was going to put them out of business. In 2009 they lost 55 percent of their fifteen thousand beehives. In 2010, after replacing their lost colonies, they suffered huge losses again—75 percent of their hives collapsed. So in November 2011, after rebuilding their colonies yet again, they didn't transport their beehives to California as they usually did at that time of year. Instead, they moved the hives into an apple storage warehouse.

In California the warm weather would have kept the bees flying. And the bees would have needed to be fed to make up for not being able to find enough flowers to meet their nectar needs. But in the dark warehouse, with the temperature at a constant 40°F (4.4°C), the bees stopped flying. And the queen took a break from rearing brood. Safe from windstorms, cold snaps, and even predators like bears and skunks, the bees rested.

The Olsons' experiment worked. "When we took the bees to the almonds at the end of January 2011," Sue said, "they were fat and healthy. And when the almond season finished that year, we'd only lost 3 percent of our hives."

Stacked eight and nine hives high, the bee colonies are having a safe, "pretend" winter inside the warehouse.

Will the Future Be Sweet?

By spring 2012, U.S. beekeepers were reporting an annual loss of only 20 percent of their hives from CCD. That was much better than the 30 to 50 percent loss reported in 2007, and scientists believed things were looking up for the bees. But by early 2013, the situation had changed. "The 2013 season may be the worst yet for CCD," reported beekeeper Dave Hackenberg.

So why are colonies still disappearing so quickly? The summer of 2012 was very dry in some parts of the United States. In those areas, the bees would have produced and stored less honey than usual for times when there wasn't any nectar source. Beekeepers also reported an increase in varroa mites in their hives in 2012. Reports of *Nosema ceranae*, though, weren't any worse. Researcher Jeff Pettis said, "These ups and downs just prove that we're still trying to get a handle on this problem, and that there's more work to be done."

Honeybees still buzz around plants and ferry pollen between flowers. But the world is becoming an unfriendly place for bees. Will honeybees ever be safe from the threat of CCD? Scientists and beekeepers are combining their efforts and continuing to work hard to make that possible. For now, though, the challenge is making sure enough honeybees survive for colonies to make it from one year to the next. The idea of honeybee colonies living free of the threat of collapse is only a dream.

There isn't any place in the world that's completely safe for honeybees—at least not yet.

43

Author's Note

No movie about tracking down killers could be more exciting than this true story. It was thrilling to search out and interview scientists who are working on this case. One of my favorite moments was talking to Gloria DeGrandi-Hoffman and hearing how excited and hopeful she was about her work. She explained how new technologies are opening up new research possibilities that could help stop CCD. Then I talked to beekeepers and became caught up in the very personal side of the story of the vanishing honeybees. Like any farmer with livestock, beekeepers care about the bees they tend. They're crushed by losing so many in a bad year. The problem is, even in a good year, honeybees are still dying. Colonies—both those tended by beekeepers and those in the wild—remain at risk of collapsing. Perhaps, one day, you'll become the science detective who finally makes the world safe for honeybees. That will also make it a healthier place for all of us.

Honeybees Are Amazing!

Scientists believe honeybees have been at work pollinating Earth's plants for over 30 million years. In fact, honey has been found in ancient Egyptian tombs. You may be amazed to learn it's still safe to eat. That's because honey contains natural preservatives that prevent bacteria from growing in it. Check out some other incredible facts about honeybees.

- Honeybees have two "stomachs." One digests food, and one holds nectar while they forage.

- Honeybee larvae don't give off wastes. So they can grow up inside a wax cell on a puddle of food and not get it dirty.

- Honeybees perform special movements called dances to let other workers know how far and what direction to fly to find food. They can give directions to supplies within about 500 feet (152 meters) of the hive.

- Honeybees produce pheromones. This lets worker bees guard the hive entrance. Any arriving bee that doesn't have the pheromone of a hive mate could be a honey thief and is attacked.

- Bees produce wax, and without any training or blueprints, bees build perfect six-sided tubelike cells. Bees also slightly angle the cells up so honey and pollen won't fall out.

Help Your Local Honeybees

Here are some things you can do that will make a big difference to your local honeybees.

- Buy local honey. That helps local beekeepers so they're able to maintain their bee colonies in your community.

- Plant with honeybees in mind. If your family plants a garden or flowerpots, choose plants whose flowers will supply bees with nectar and pollen. Check with your local plant nursery to find out what's best to plant in your area. In the United States, download the free pollinator-friendly planting guide for your area. It's available from the Pollinator Partnership (http:// pollinator.org/index.html). Keep in mind that bees are especially attracted to blue, purple, and yellow flowers.

- Let weeds grow until their flowers are finished blooming. Bees benefit from having access to dandelions and clover. Even more important is to not use pesticides on grass and weeds.

- Encourage your school and local community to leave areas for plants around playgrounds and parking lots. You can also suggest they choose landscaping plants, even if they're only potted plants, with bees in mind.

Global Rescue Efforts

Check out these worldwide efforts to help honeybees. You and your family may want to join one of these or put one of these ideas into action in your community.

British Beekeepers Association Adopt a Beehive Project: In Britain, people are making donations to help support local beekeepers in their efforts to raise healthy bees. Those who join Adopt a Beehive receive a jar of honey, a pack of pollinator-friendly wildflower seeds to plant, information about honeybees, and regular updates on their hives.

Pollinator Week: This event isn't just for bees. It's a week to hold events supporting the good health of all the natural pollinators: bees, birds, butterflies, bats, and other insects, such as beetles. The U.S. Senate voted five years ago to make the last week in June National Pollinator Week. Many states as well as Canada hold activities to encourage people to think globally and act locally to provide adequate sources of pollen and nectar for their community pollinators.

Trees for Bees: BeeAlive (http://www. beealive.com/), a company supplying royal jelly-based health supplements, is supporting customers and local communities in planting fruit trees. The company's immediate goal is for one million fruit trees. The company's goal is to establish a long-lasting source of pollen and nectar for honeybees.

Glossary

beebread: a combination of pollen mixed with honey. It is an important food for bees, helping them stay healthy and strong.

brood: the developing young bees

Colony Collapse Disorder (CCD): the name given to an unknown combination of factors that cause so many worker bees to abandon the hive that the colony dies

drone bee: a male bee raised to mate with any newly emerged queen bee

egg: the beginning stage of a bee's life

forager: a worker bee that leaves the hive to collect nectar and honey to carry back to the hive

fungus: a plantlike living thing that, unlike a plant, cannot make its own food. It feeds off another living thing. Types of fungi include yeasts and bread molds.

larva: a grublike immature bee. It hatches from an egg and leads up to the pupal stage.

nectar: a sweet liquid produced by flowers to attract pollinators

neonicotinoid pesticide: a kind of insecticide (substance that kills insects) that was developed based on the naturally occurring chemicals in a tobacco plant's leaves

Nosema ceranae: a fungus that affects the digestive tract of bees

pesticide: a chemical used to kill insects or other living things that are considered problems

pheromone: a chemical given off by an individual animal to affect the behavior of other individuals of the same animal group

pollen: the male reproductive cells in flowers

pollination: the process of pollen being moved from the male part of a flower to the female part of a flower

pupa: the stage of a bee's life when it changes from a larva to an adult

queen bee: a female bee that is able to produce offspring for the colony

royal jelly: a secretion from a special part on a nurse bee's head. It is fed to all larvae for the first two days of their lives. A larva being raised to become a queen bee continues to be fed royal jelly. An adult queen bee is also fed royal jelly.

varroa mite: a tiny relative of a spider that attaches itself to a honeybee and lives by sucking the honeybee's body fluids. This mite may also inject disease-causing viruses into its bee host.

virus: a tiny living thing that is unable to grow and reproduce unless it's living inside a host's cells. Many viruses cause changes in the host's body that make the host sick.

worker bee: a female bee that is unable to produce offspring. Depending on its age, the worker bee performs different jobs for the colony.

Digging Deeper

To keep on investigating honeybees, explore these books and websites:

Books
Burns, Loree Griffin. *The Hive Detectives.* Boston: Houghton Mifflin Books for Children, 2010.
How do beekeepers keep from getting stung? And how exactly do people study vanishing bees? This book answers these questions and more, giving a closer look at how scientists began investigating CCD.

Editors of Time for Kids. *Time for Kids Bees.* New York: HarperCollins, 2005.
Vivid, close-up photos take you inside a hive for an in-depth look at the members of a honeybee colony.

Kalman, Bobbie. *What Is Pollination?* New York: Crabtree Publishing, 2010.
Investigate the pollination process in this book. Learn more about bees' role and why pollination is so important.

Nargi, Lela. *The Honeybee Man.* New York: Schwartz & Wade, 2011.
Follow the story of a beekeeper in Brooklyn, New York, who tends three hives on his rooftop! This illustrated story provides a fun glimpse into beekeeping.

Websites
Honey: National Honey Board
http://www.honey.com
You know that honey is deliciously sweet, but did you know that it's good for your skin? It can help your sore throat too! Explore this site for more amazing facts about honey.

Kidzone: Ontario Beekeepers Association
http://www.ontariobee.com/index.php?action=display&cat=38
Check out this page to learn how fast honeybees can fly, how many eyes they have (more than two!), how they weatherproof their hives, and more. Don't miss the Activities & Puzzles page!

NATURE: Silence of the Bees—Inside the Hive
http://www.youtube.com/watch?v=lE-8QuBDkkw
This short video from PBS takes you inside a beehive for an up-close look at the amazing, crowded life in a colony.

Index

Photo Acknowledgments

The images in this book are used with the permission of: © Alle/Dreamstime.com, pp. 1, 3, 4 (top), 6 (top), 16, 30, 42, 44, 47; AP Photo/Jimmy May, p. 4 (bottom); © Kathy Keatley Garvey, pp. 5, 12 (top), 20, 38–39, 43; © Andrey Kiselev/Dreamstime.com, p. 6 (bottom); © Laura Westlund/Independent Picture Service, pp. 7 (top), 19; © Stockbyte/Getty Images, p. 7 (bottom); © Minden Pictures/SuperStock, pp. 8, 12 (bottom center), 29 (bottom); © Michael Maloney/San Francisco Chronicle/CORBIS, p. 9; © Maria Stenzel/National Geographic/Getty Images, pp. 10–11, 38; © Ralph Orlowski/Getty Images, p. 11; © Eric Tourneret/Visuals Unlimited, Inc., pp. 12 (bottom left and bottom right), 18, 31, 33; © W. Treat Davidson/Photo Researchers, Inc., p. 14 (top); © Scott Camazine & Kirk Visscher/Photo Researchers, Inc., p. 14 (bottom); © Bjorn Holland/Photodisc/Getty Images, pp. 14–15; © Nazabb/ Dreamstime.com, pp. 16–17; © Radius Images/Getty Images, p. 17; © Richard Clark/Garden Picture Library/Getty Images, p. 21; © Nicholas Kamm/AFP/Getty Images, p. 23; Agricultural Research Service, USDA, pp. 24–25, 34–35; © Scott Camazine/Photo Researchers, Inc., p. 26; © Robin Loznak/ZUMA Press/CORBIS, p. 27; © Philip Wallick/age fotostock/Getty Images, p. 29 (top); © David Addison/Visuals Unlimited, Inc., p. 32; © Ann Johansson/CORBIS, p. 34; © Alastair Miller/Bloomberg/Getty Images, p. 36; © Paul J. Richards/AFP/Getty Images, p. 37; © Ericcrama/ Dreamstime.com, p. 41.

Cover photographs © NHPA/SuperStock (main); © Alle/Dreamstime.com (jacket flap).